Chorale Preludes for Manuals

Johann Sebastian Bach

Book One

Kevin Mayhew

Extracted from

The Complete Organ Works of J S Bach

Executive Editor	Alan Ridout
Managing Editor	Anthea Smith
Music Setting	Christopher Hinkins

This compilation first published in Great Britain in 1995 by
KEVIN MAYHEW LTD
Rattlesden
Bury St Edmunds
Suffolk IP30 0SZ

ISBN 0 86209 607 3
Catalogue No: 1400043

Printed and bound in Hong Kong

Contents

Ach Herr, mich armen Sünder

BWV 742

* These appear as Oberwerk (I) and Rückpositiv (II) in the earliest source.

Alle Menschen müssen sterben

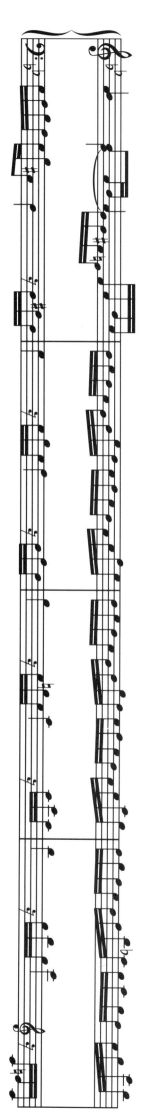

BWV 1117

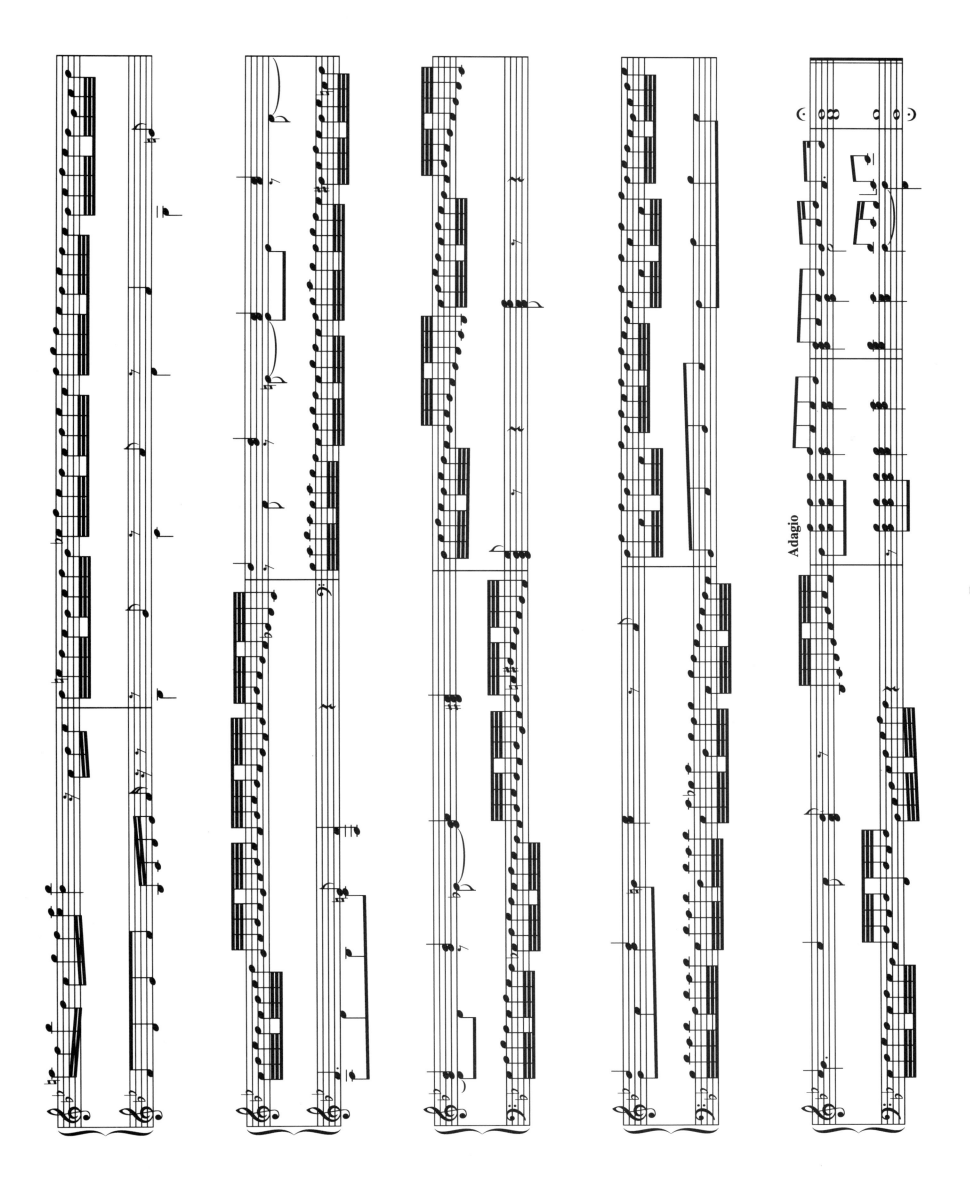

Adagio

Allein Gott in der Höh' sei Ehr'

BWV 675

a 3 / canto fermo in alto

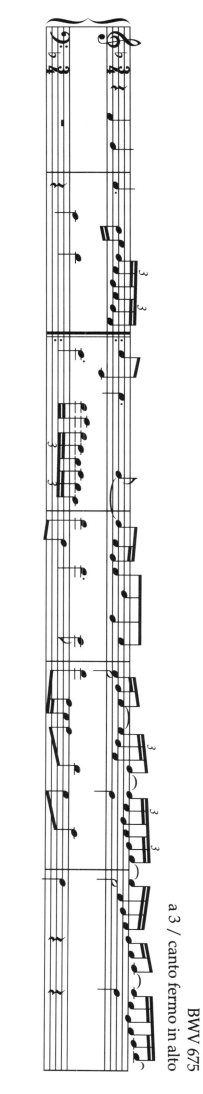

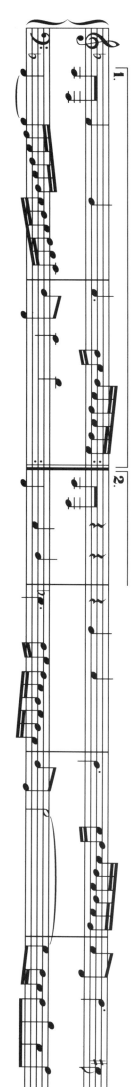

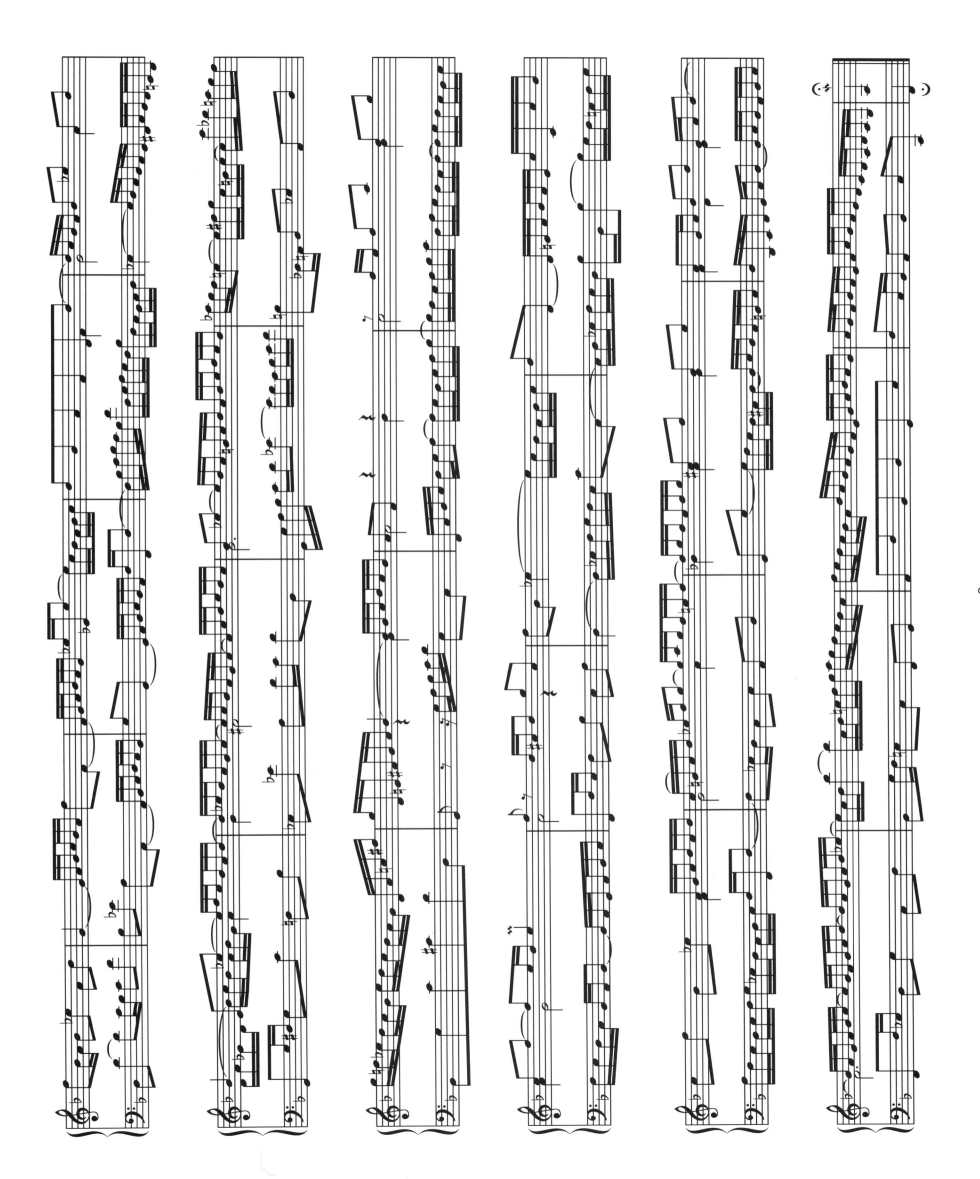

Johann Sebastian Bach

Allein Gott in der Höh' sei Ehr'

BWV 677
manualiter

Allein Gott in der Höh' sei Ehr'

BWV 711
bicinium

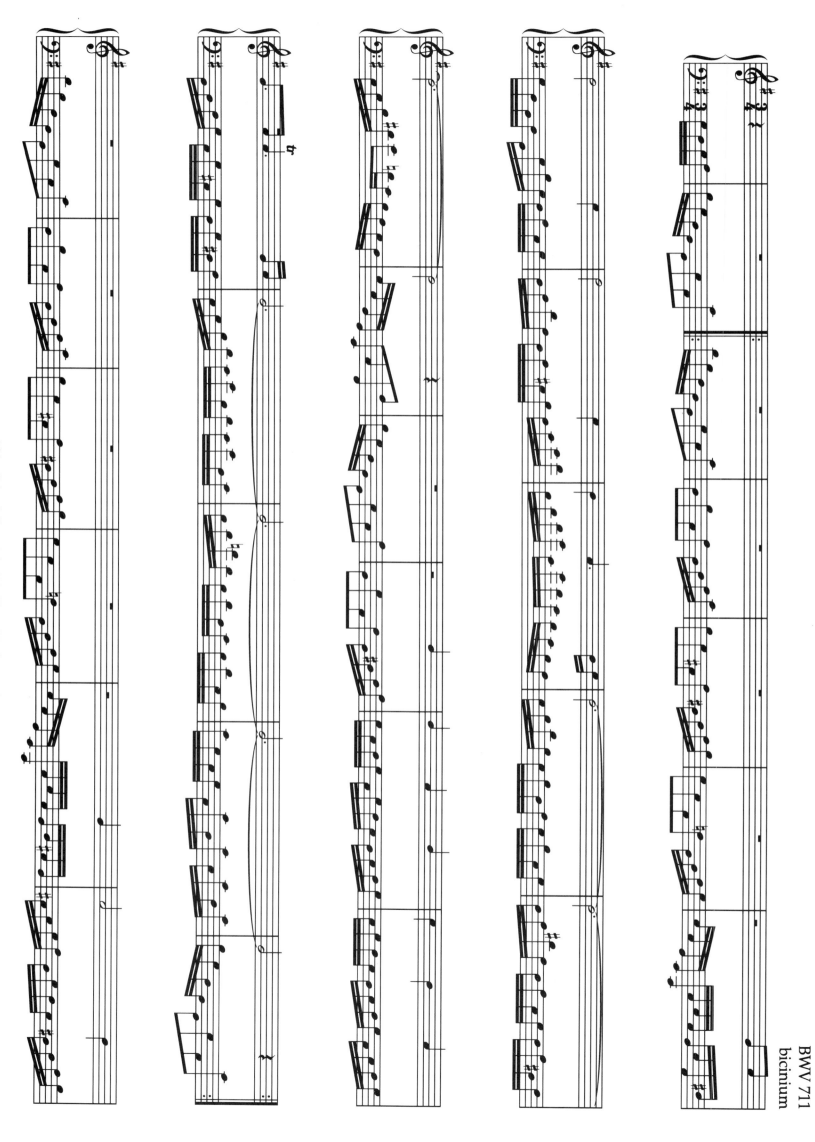

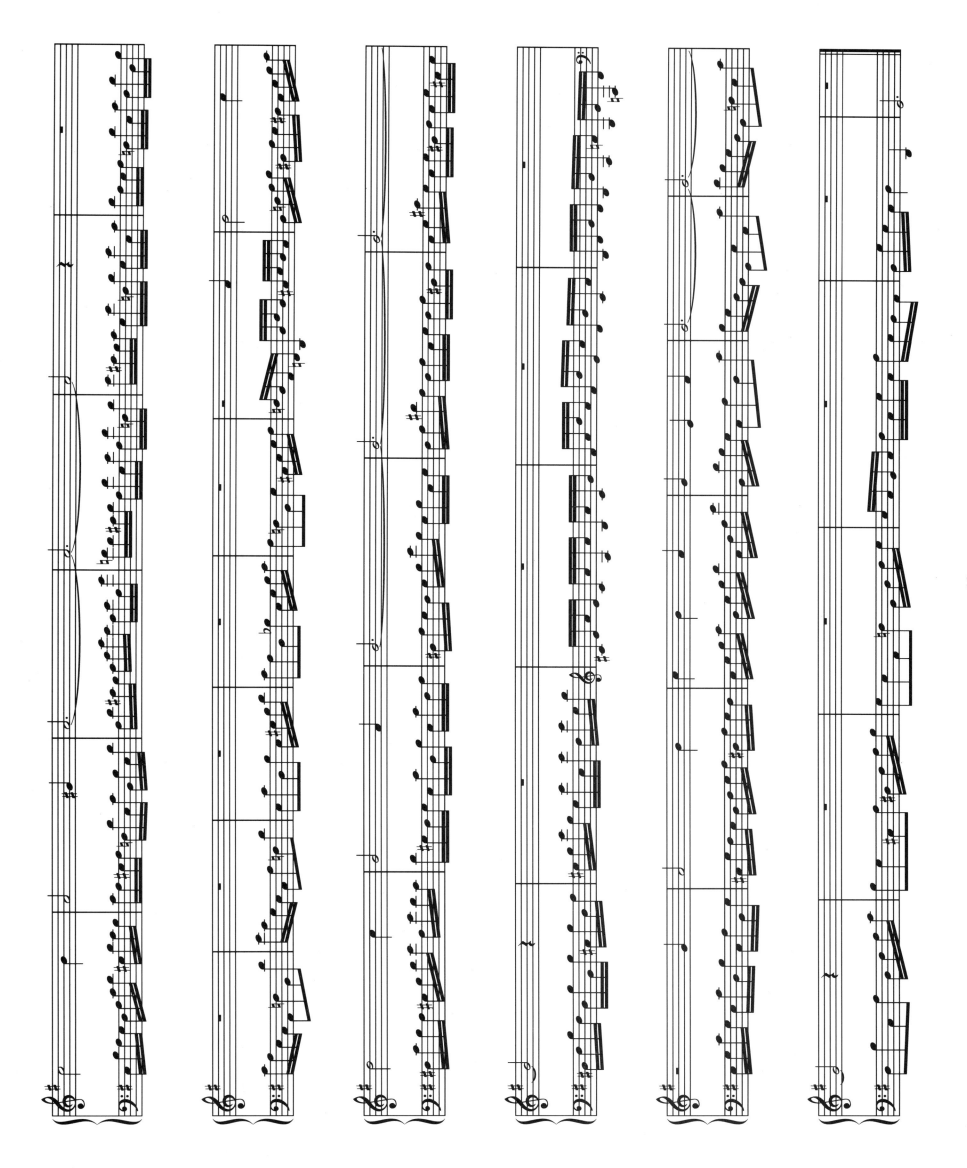

13

Allein Gott in der Höh' sei Ehr'

BWV 717
manualiter

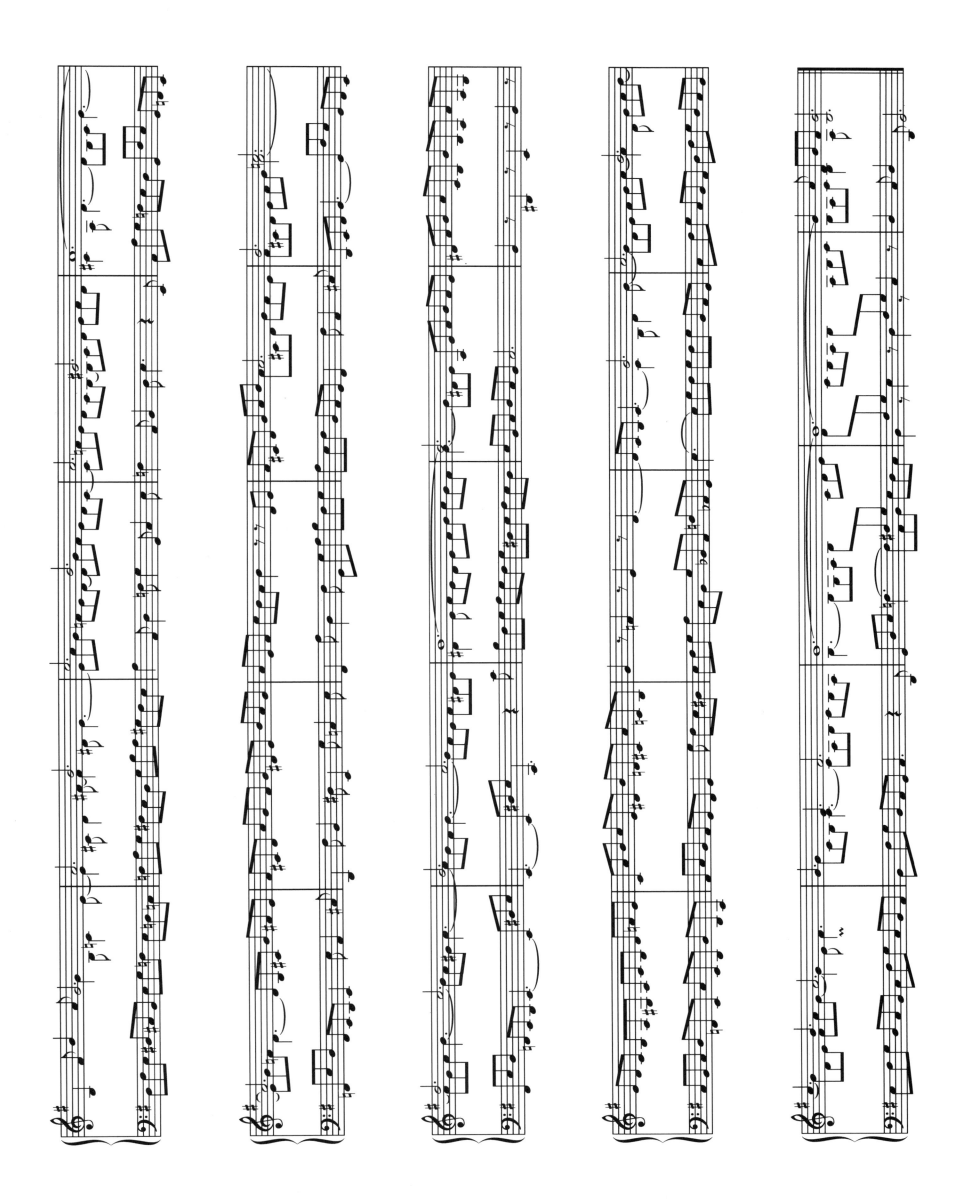

Allein zu dir, Herr Jesu Christ

BWV 1100

17

Aus tiefer Not schrei ich zu dir

BWV 687
manualiter
a 4 / alio modo

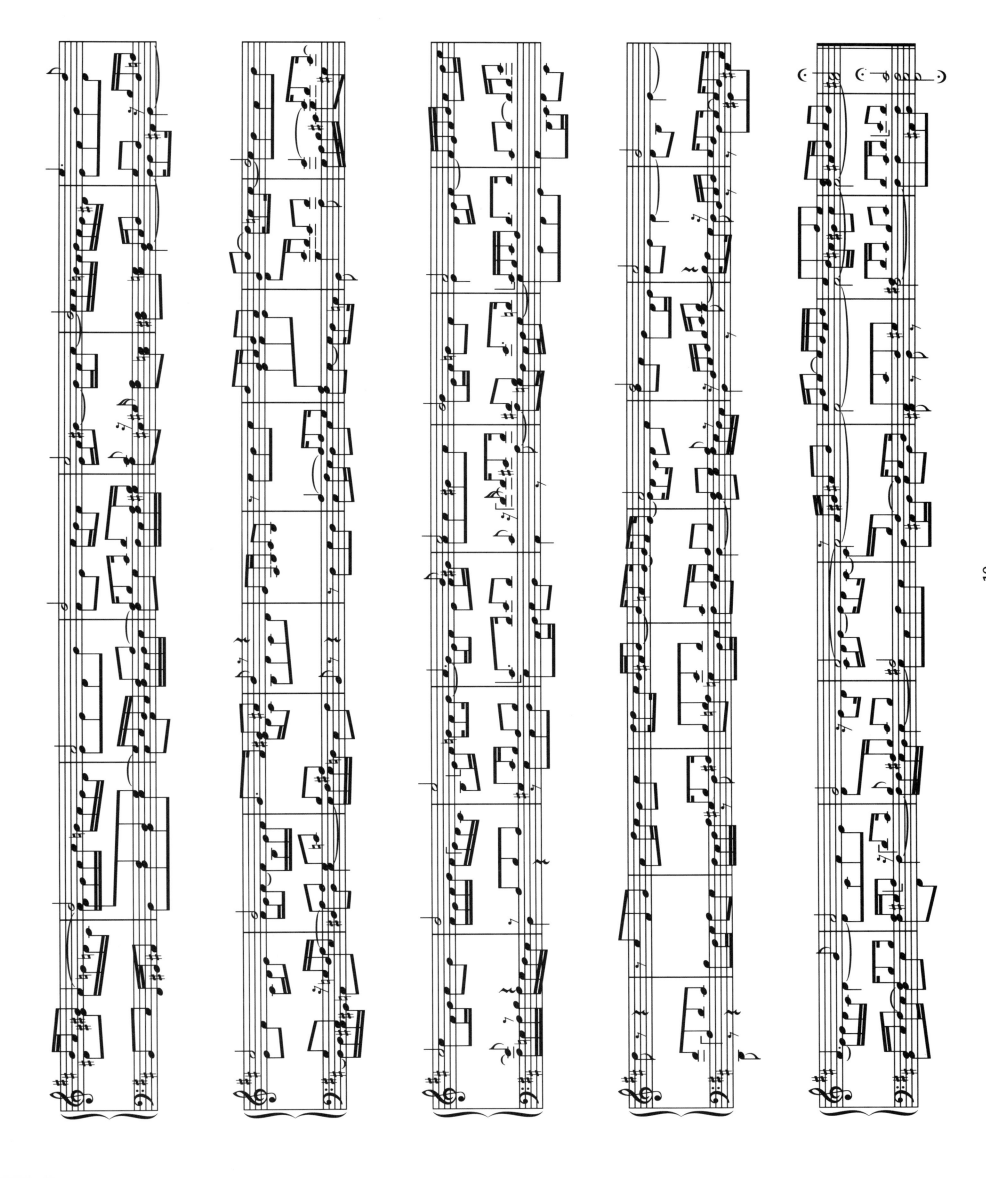

Christ lag in Todesbanden

BWV 695
manualiter
choralis in alto

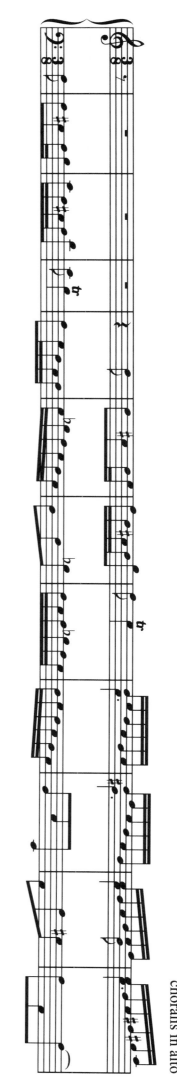

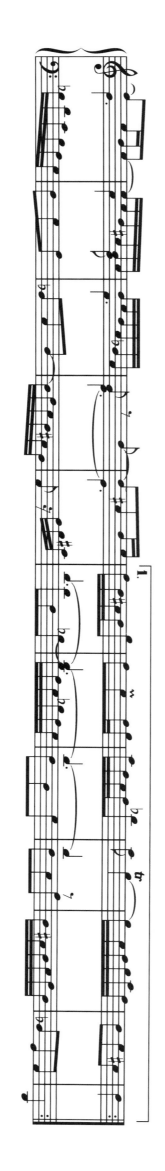
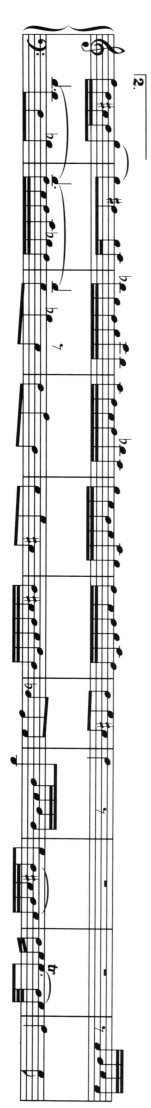

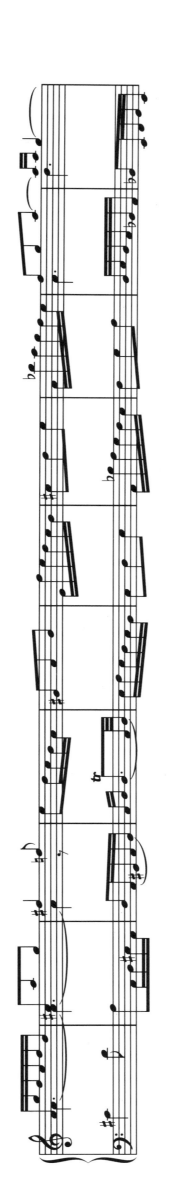
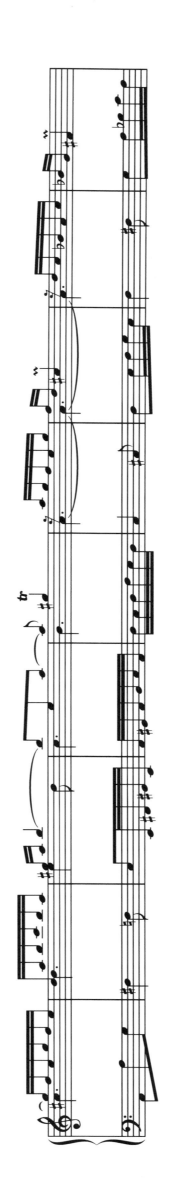
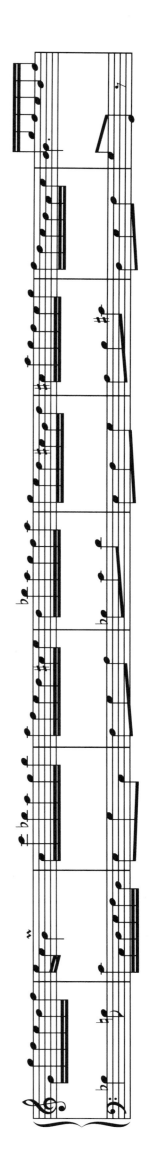

21

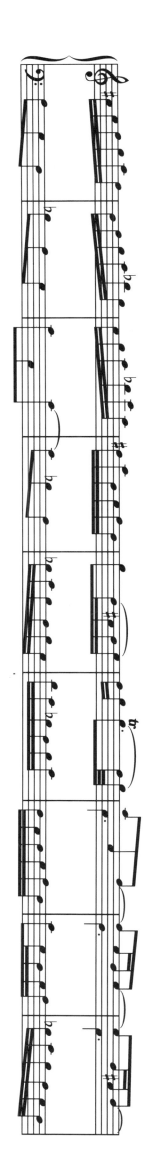
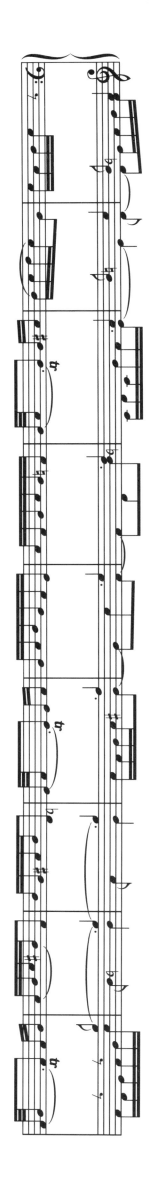

Christ, unser Herr, zum Jordan kam

BWV 685
manualiter
alio modo

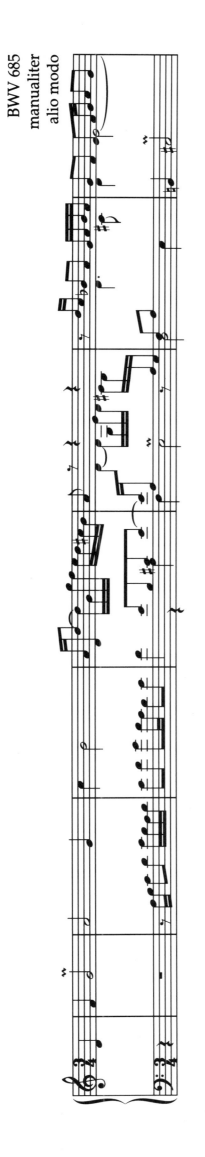
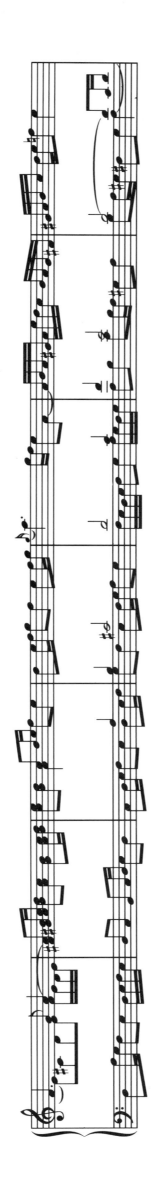

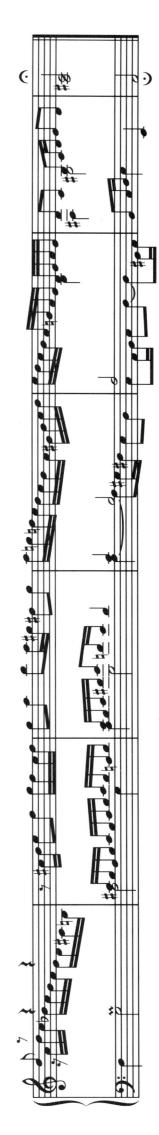

23

Christe, der du bist Tag und Licht
(Wir danken dir, Herr Jesu Christ)

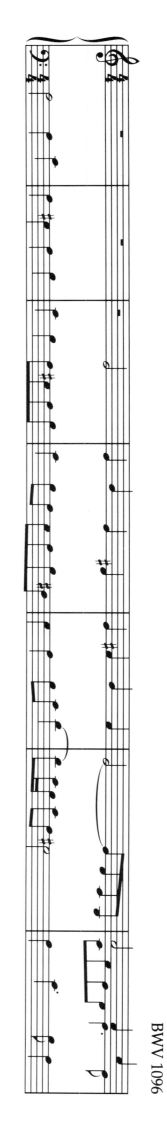

BWV 1096

Christe, aller Welt Trost

BWV 673

26

Christum wir sollen loben schon

BWV 696
manualiter
fughetta

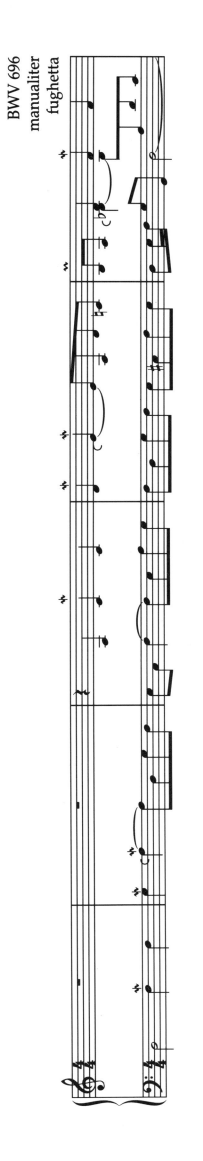
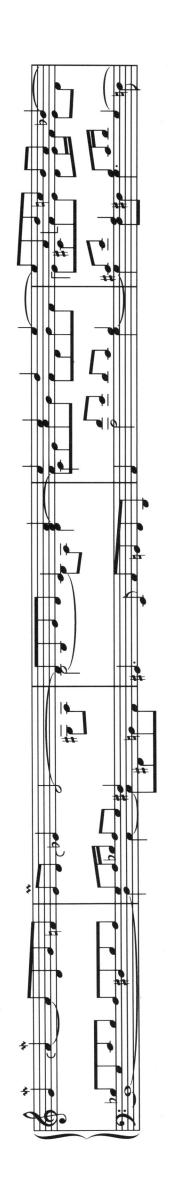
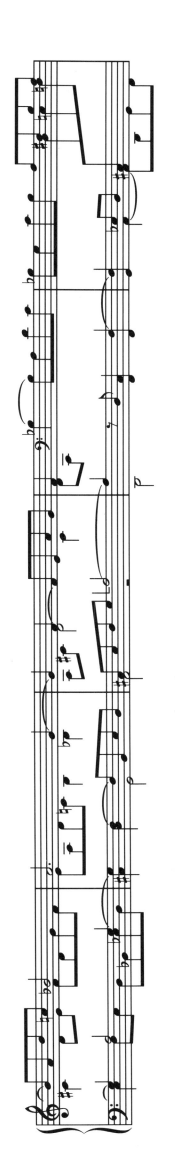
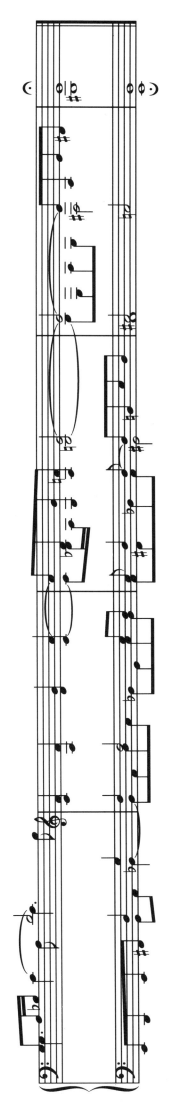

27

Christus, der ist mein Leben

BWV 1112

Das alte Jahr vergangen ist

BWV 1091

Der Tag, der ist so freudenreich
(Ein Kindelein so löbelich)

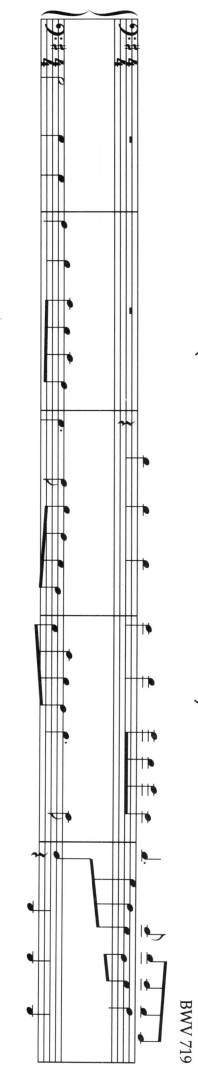

BWV 719

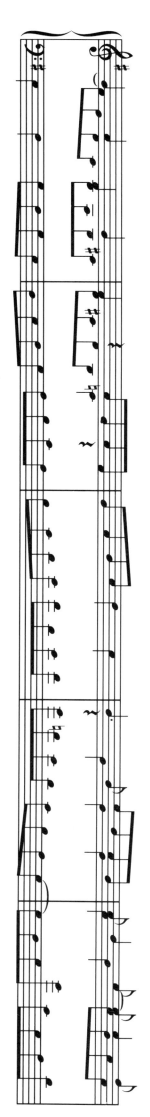

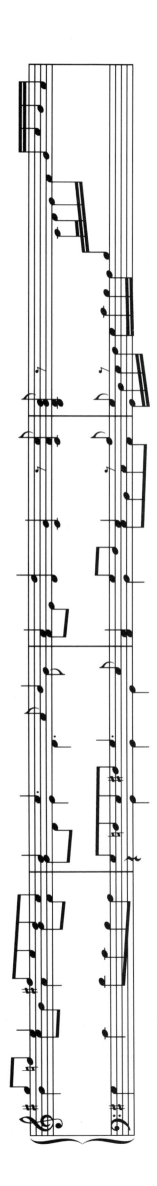
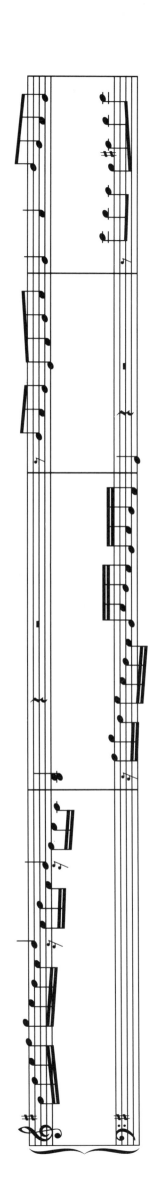
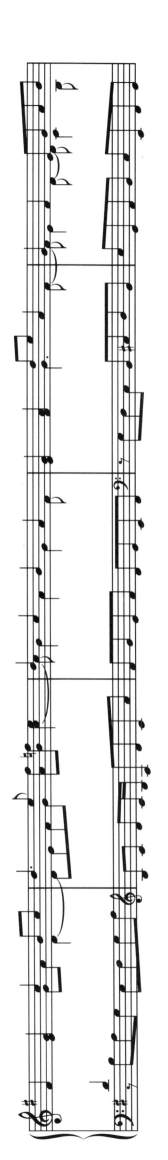
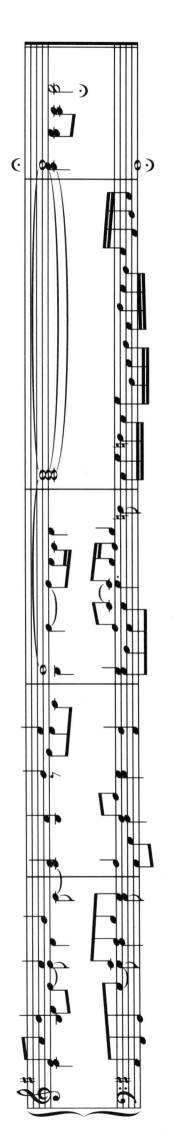

31

Dies sind die heil'gen zehn Gebot

BWV 679
manualiter

32

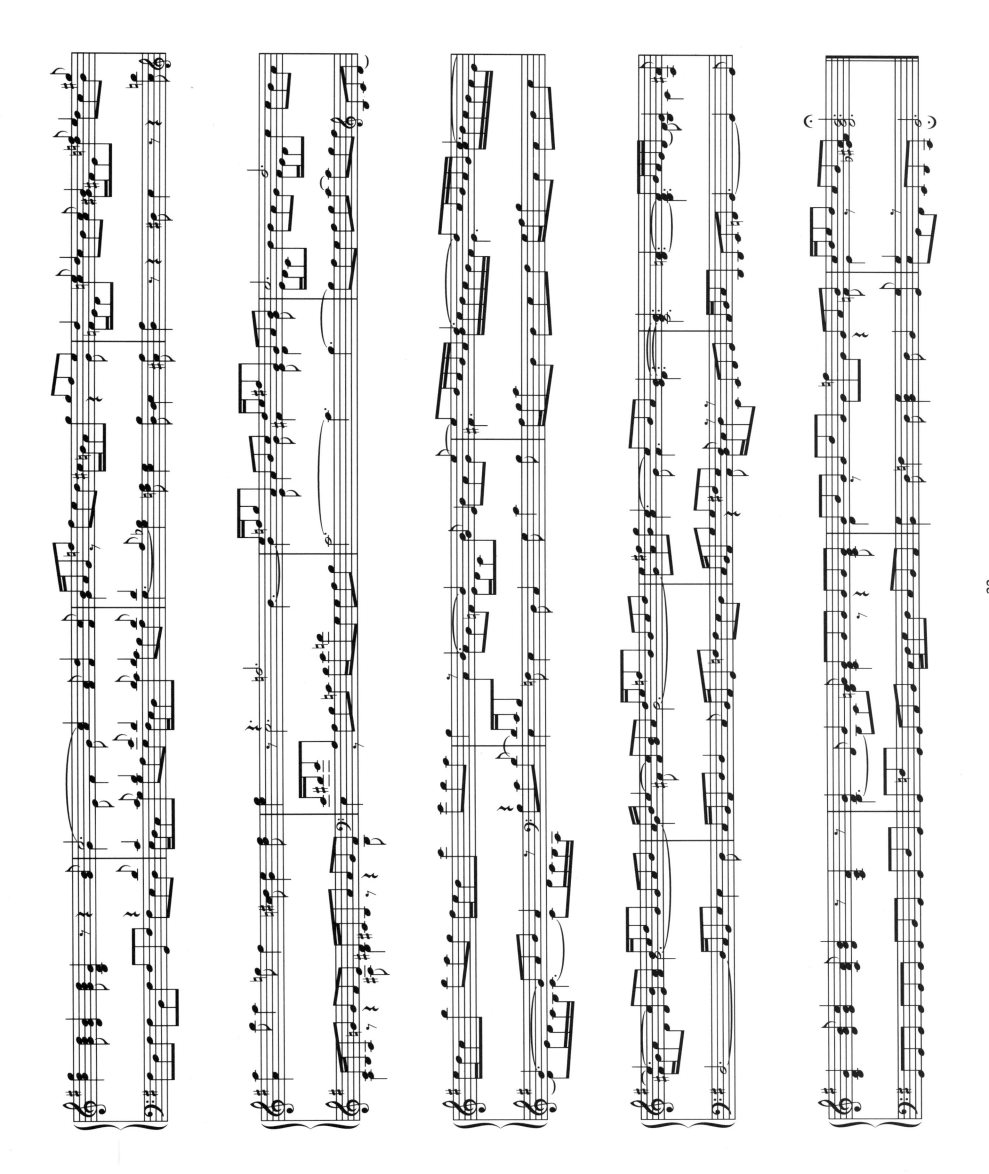

Du Friedefürst, Herr Jesu Christ

34

BWV 1102

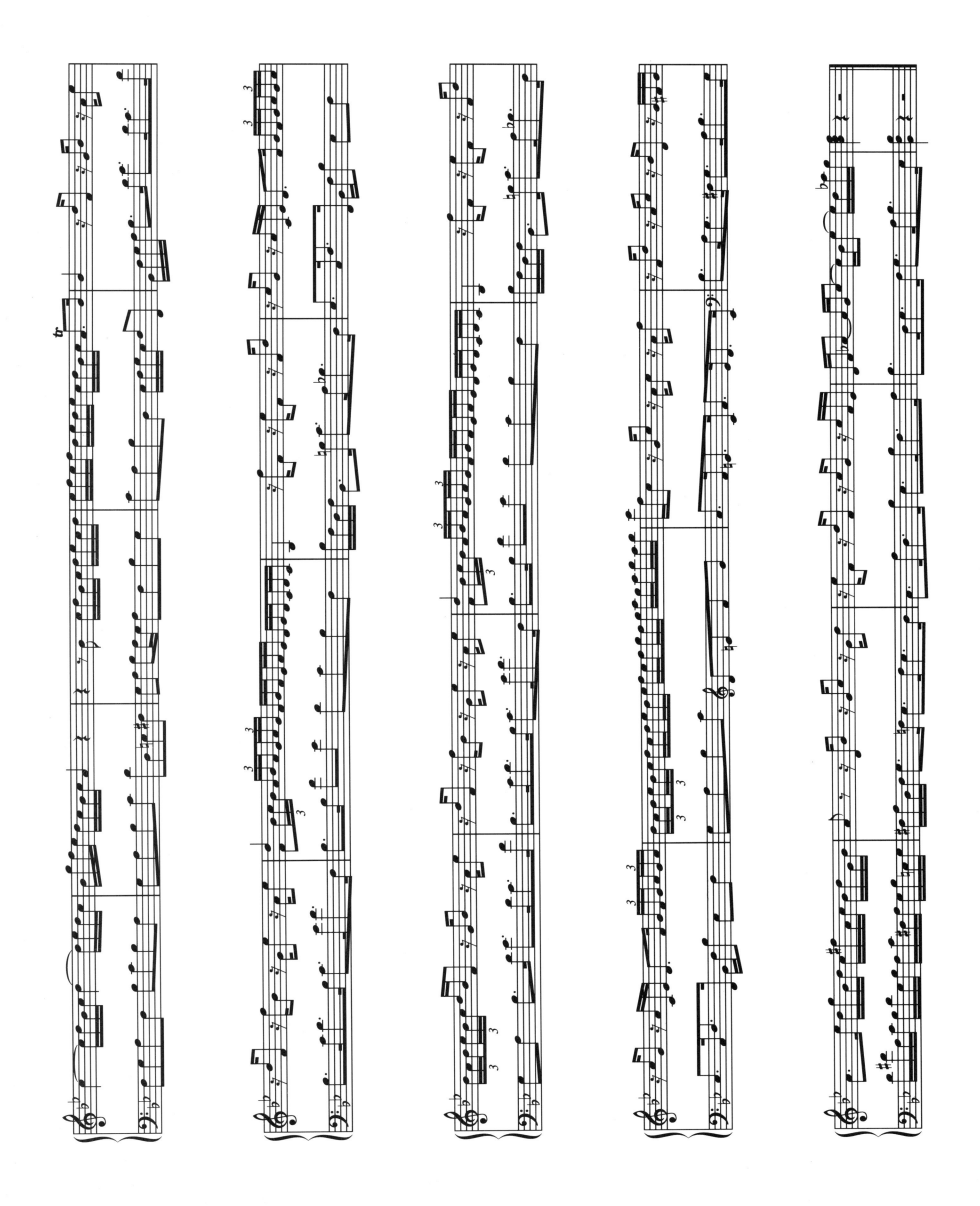

Durch Adams Fall ist ganz verderbt

BWV 1101

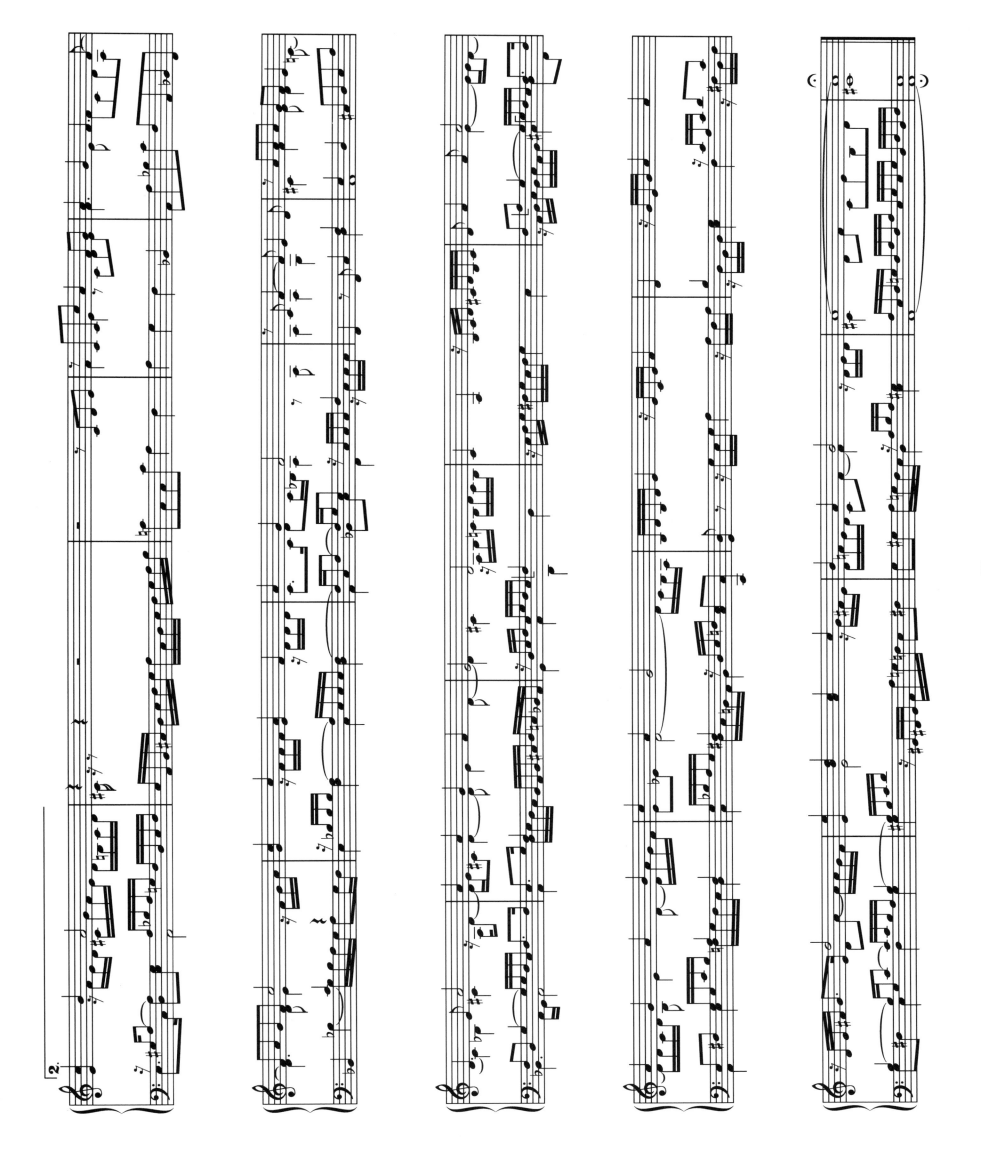

Ehre sei dir, Christe, der du leidest Not

BWV 1097

Erbarm' dich mein, O Herre Gott

BWV 721
manualiter

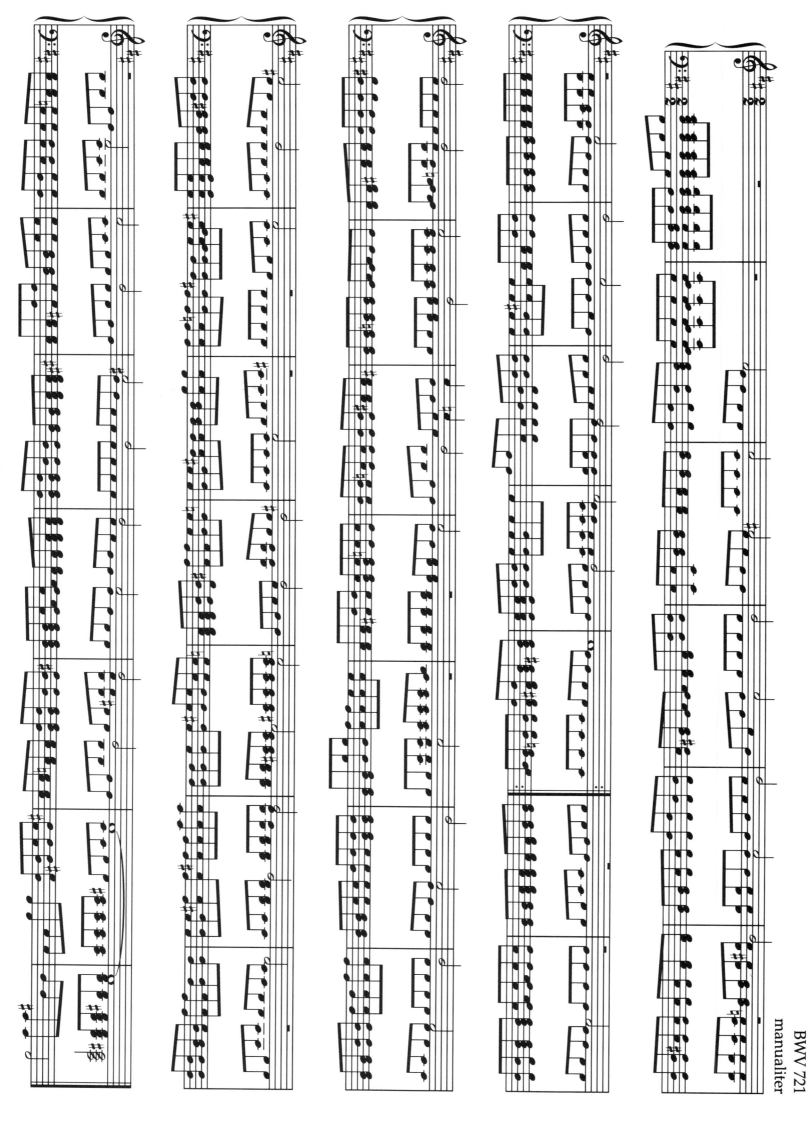

Erhalt uns, Herr, bei deinem Wort

BWV 1103

41

Gelobet seist du, Jesu Christ

BWV 697
manualiter
fughetta

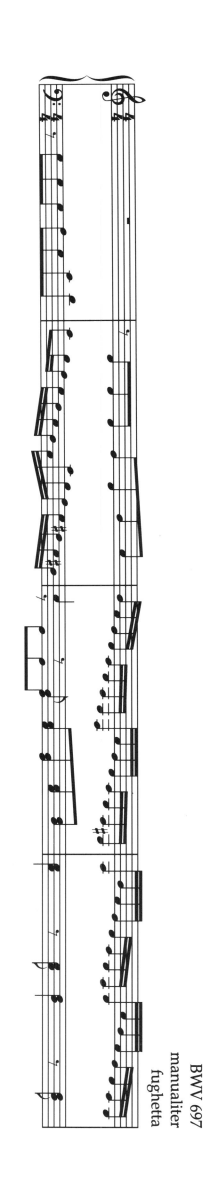
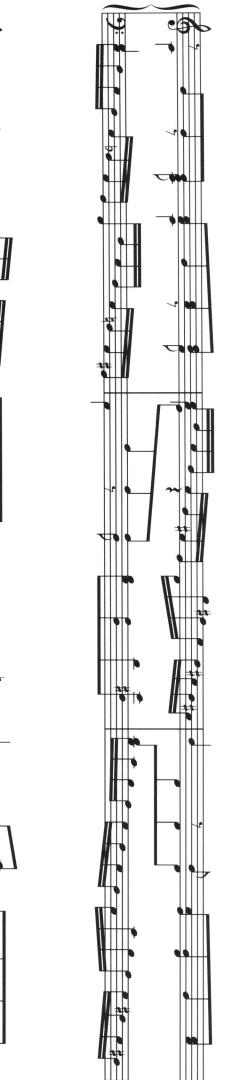
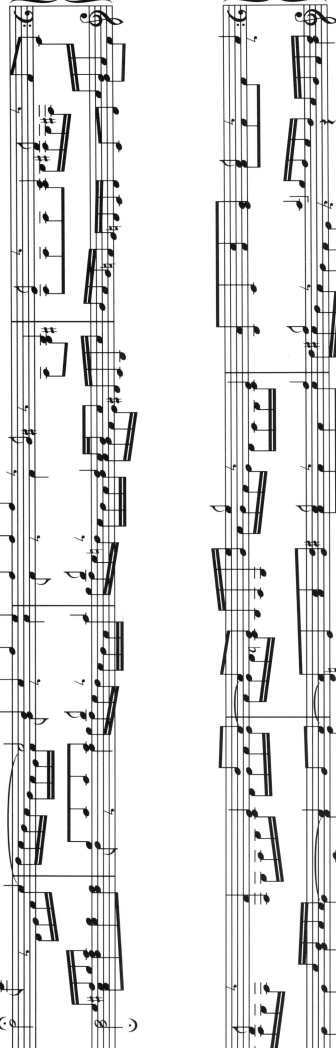

Gelobet seist du, Jesu Christ

Gott ist mein Heil, mein Hilf und Trost

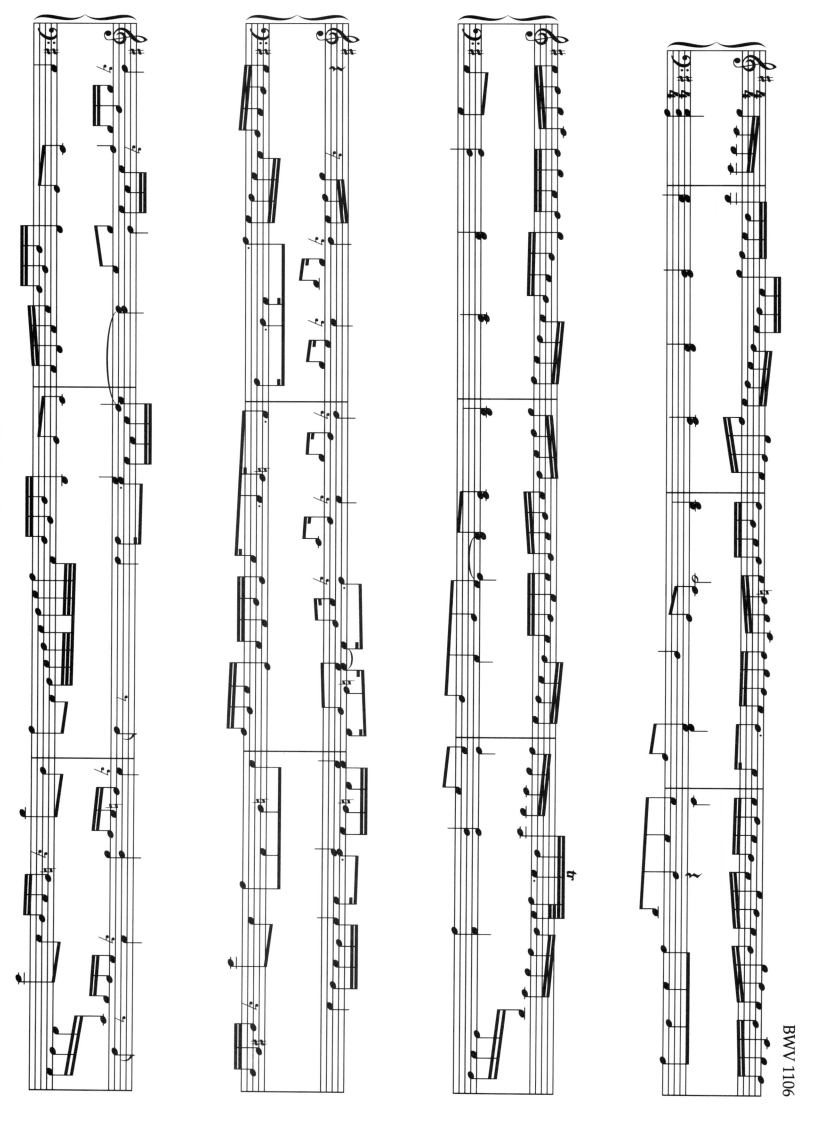

BWV 1106

45

Gottes Sohn ist kommen

BWV 703
manualiter
fughetta

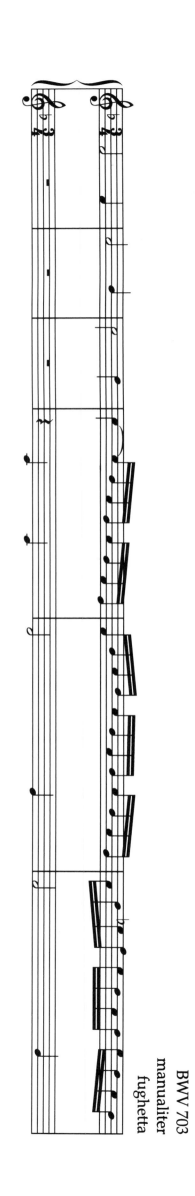
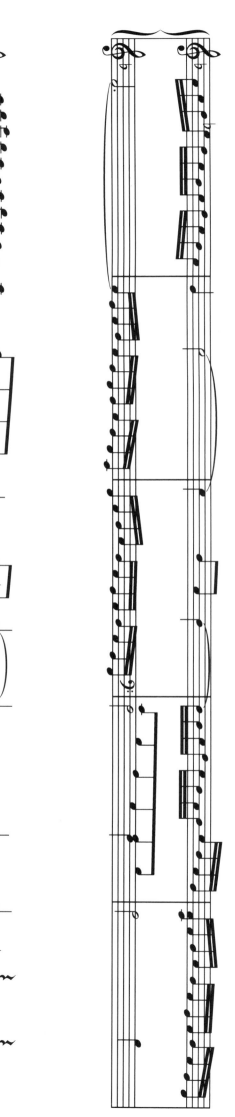

Herr Christ, der ein'ge Gottes-Sohn

BWV 698
manualiter
fughetta

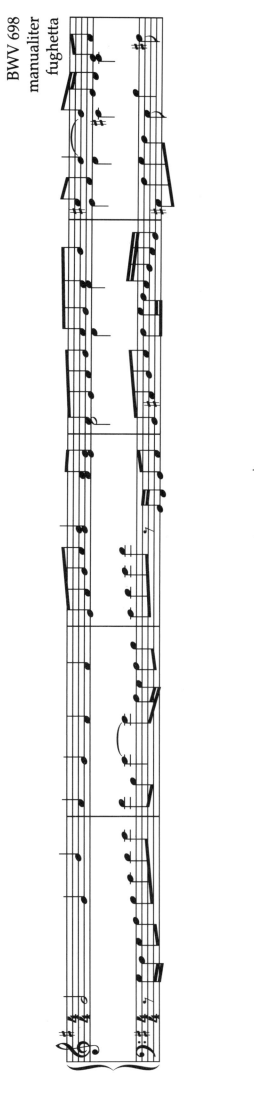
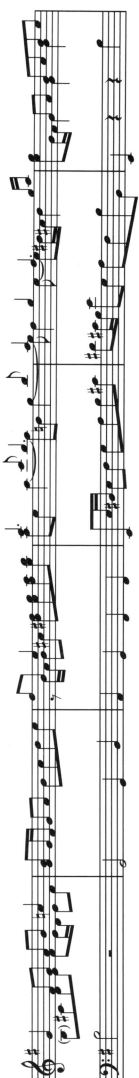
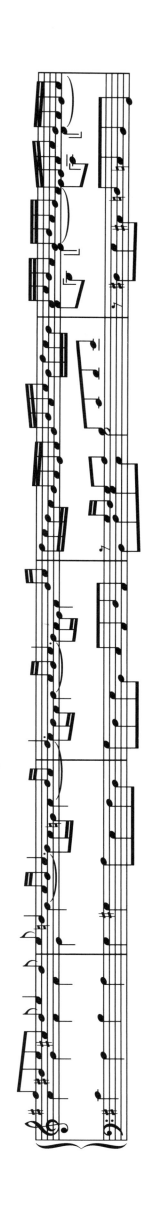
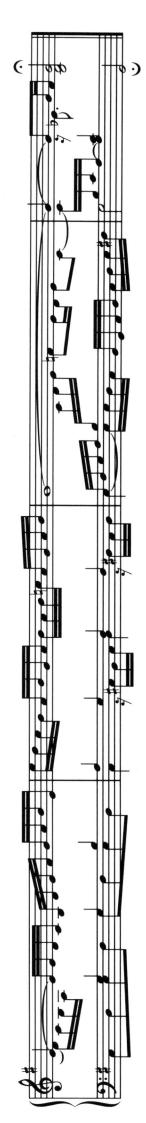

Herr Gott, nun schleuß den Himmel auf

BWV 1092

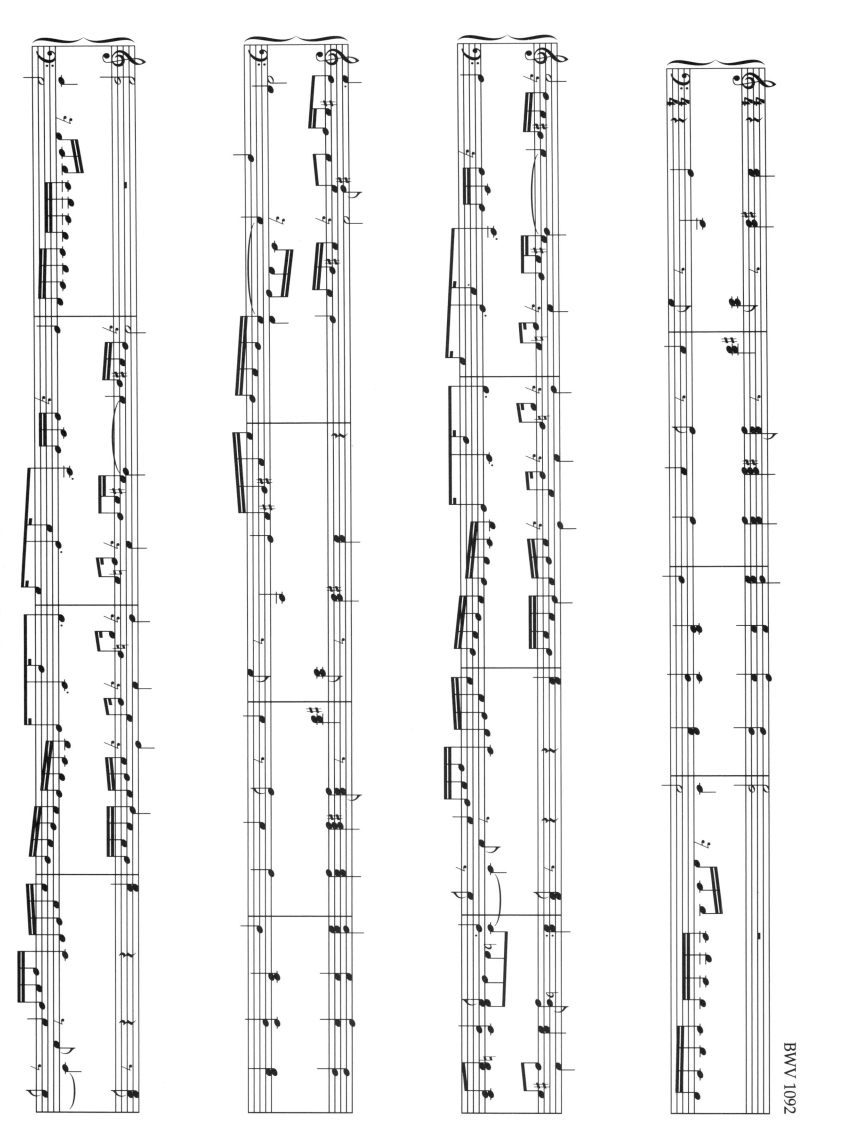

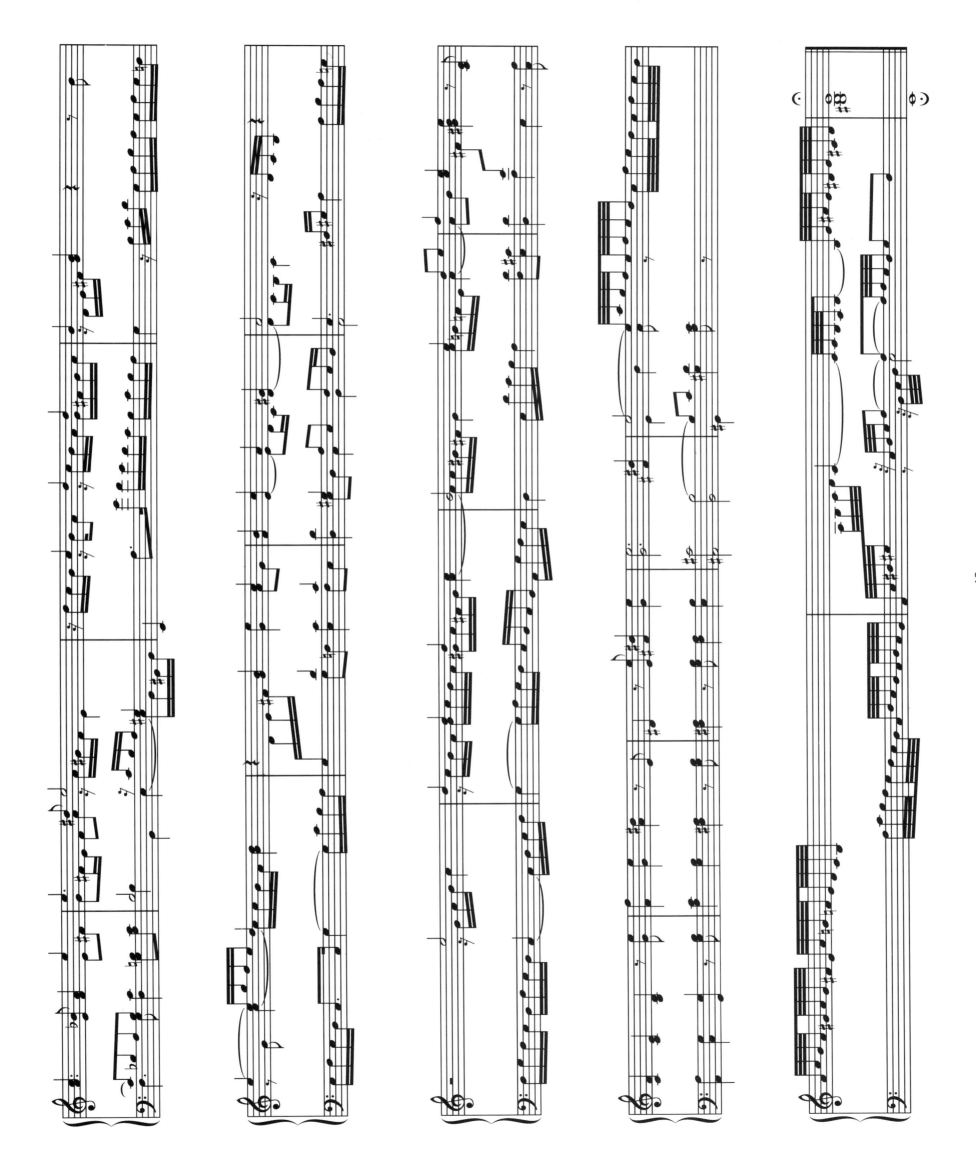

49

Herr Jesu Christ, du höchstes Gut

BWV 1114

50

Herzlich lieb hab ich dich, O Herr

BWV 1115

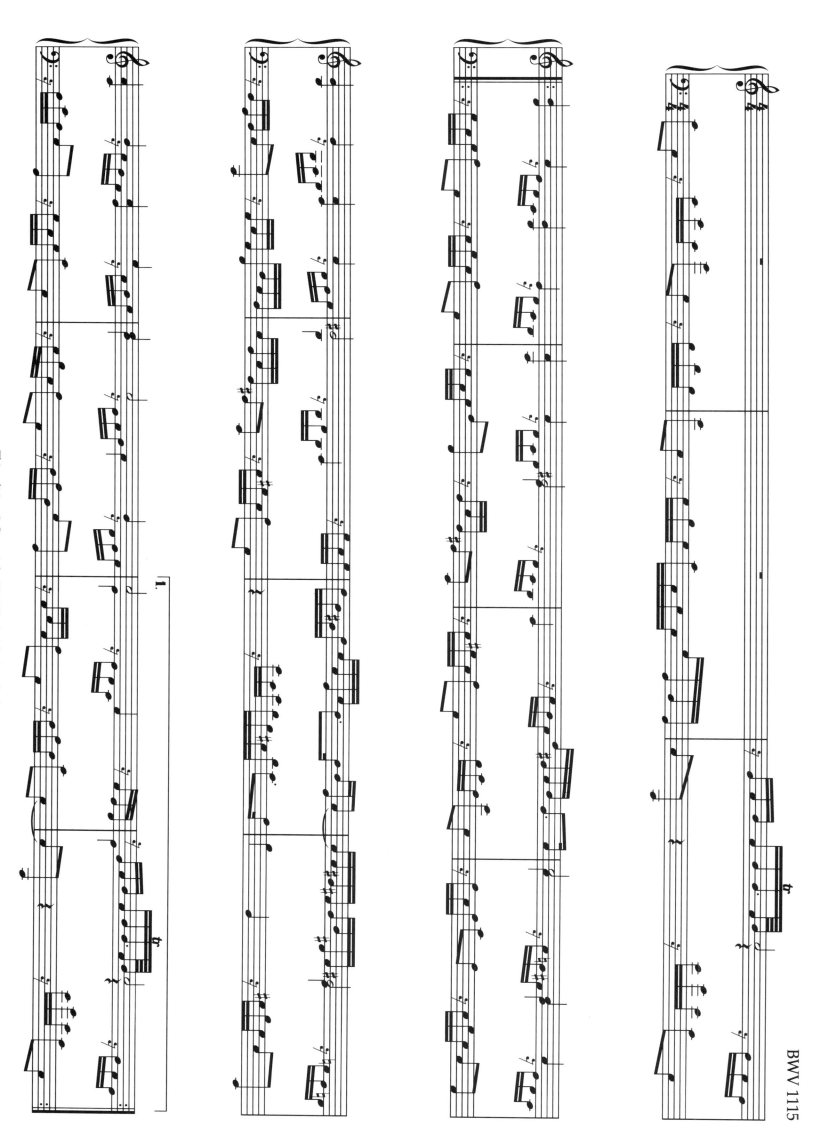

52

53

Herzliebster Jesu, was hast du verbrochen

BWV 1093

54

Ornamentation

J S Bach himself left one indicator on ornamentation in the form of a table of thirteen ornaments and their written-out equivalents for his ten-year-old son, Wilhelm Friedemann. It is given here without the brief verbal descriptions which in many cases are now either obsolete or actually misleading.

It is tempting to exaggerate the importance of this list coming, as it does, from the hand of the master and for an instructional purpose. There are problems to it as it is applied to specific music; and it is not comprehensive. Yet to focus too assiduously on the problems is probably to underestimate its importance. So long as it is taken as a general guide and not as an infallible statement it will prove very useful.

ALAN RIDOUT

'Explanation of various signs, showing how to play certain ornaments neatly'

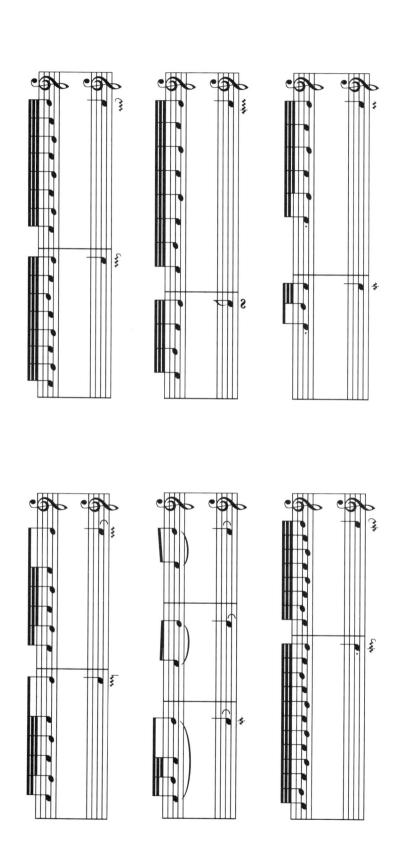